Dedication

This book is dedicated to my beginner, intermediate, and experienced investors for their passion and dedication for real estate and their businesses. I would like to personally thank my mother for all of her support, my lovely group of friends who are always pushing me and motivating me. My brother from another mother and business partner Sayam, his wife Nichole and his family for helping me as well as my mentors including Charles Blair with the Real Deal Meetup and Mastermind family. His wisdom has been exponential to my growth and I am forever grateful.

Table of Contents

Brittney is the founder and owner of Top Notch Property Solutions, Inc. and Top Notch Holdings, LLC, two premier real estate companies located in Washington, D.C. Brittney was first introduced to the real estate industry during her time as a Special Education Teacher in Southeast D.C. Aiding in her students' families' issues with housing led her to starting her own real estate business. She quickly learned that she enjoyed real estate and helping people, and decided to make it her full-time job. She is now helping families with their troubles and made six figures flipping properties in four different states in one year.

Brittney has spoken to hundreds of people on the subject of real estate investing and shared her story and journey about quitting a full-time job to pursue her dreams of owning her own business. She was recently interviewed on the Real Deal Meetup radio show, Duru Interviews, featured in IVY magazine as Entrepreneur of the Month, and had one of her rehabs spotlighted on Fox 28 Good Day Marketplace in Columbus, OH.

She recently founded and is the owner of Top Notch Consulting, LLC, a company designed to help business owners automate their business using virtual assistants. As a result of personally consulting with top real estate investors and other small business owners, Brittney has developed a webinar training series, which has just been released to the public.

With her real estate business running on autopilot, Brittney currently serves on the Board of Trustees for Democracy Prep Public Schools in Southeast D.C. In addition, she is the Fundraising Chair and Secretary for the National Association for the Advancement of Colored People (NAACP), D.C. Branch. She would like to pursue her Executive MBA in the upcoming year and is passionate about moving into the commercial sector in her business.

Brittney works with individual students as well as runs a group-coaching program for real estate and business automation. Her one-day boot camp, held every year in Baltimore and Ft. Lauderdale is Brittney's chance to meet her students, old and new, and share her love and knowledge of real estate.

Brittney resides in Washington D.C. In her spare time she enjoys traveling the world, spin-cycling, volunteering, coaching, and spending time with family.

Introduction

The term "entrepreneur" as we know it is someone who starts and organizes a business. People are infatuated by the idea behind this term because it supposedly comes with a lifestyle that everyone dreams of having. We automatically think that as an entrepreneur you are flying around the world, working whenever you want, and—everyone's personal favorite—not having a boss or someone to report to. For some of you who have bought real estate courses and attended seminars, we see real people who are successful in real estate and dream of having that lifestyle and level of success.

Whether you are a newbie jumping into the business, trying to do this business while having another job/career, or a seasoned investor who does this full time, the real estate business is a tough one to navigate. Those who are successful simply have systems in place. While I fit the current definition of an entrepreneur, I will know I am in true "Entrepreneur Land" when I have to do no work in my business to make money. I should be able to go backpacking in Europe for a month and the amount of money that hits my account before I left should still hit my account when I get home. I'm in the process of doing that as each flip provides money for me to accumulate passive income properties. But I, too, have a ways to go.

To live that life we have to climb the ladder as outlined in the book *The E-Myth Revisited* by Michael Gerber. You are first the technician, then the manager, and then an actual entrepreneur. I'm willing to bet that the majority of you reading this book are in the technician phase of your business where you are literally doing anything and everything to make it. You are the receptionist, accountant, marketer, project manager, acquisitions manager, and maybe even the contractor, and the lender!

This book is going to give you a harsh reality check as to where you are on the ladder towards entrepreneurship in your real estate business. Now, that being said (aren't you glad I got the harsh reality stuff out of the way first?), there are many ways for you to start to fire yourself from these clerical or "technician" tasks so that you can, in fact, focus on living the life and dream of an entrepreneur and your business can run whether you decide to come to the office or you are off in Paris like I was.

Luckily for you, we are moving to a time where many people would love to work from home doing virtual jobs and, on the flipside, the majority of our real estate business can in fact be outsourced to someone else. This book gives you the insight on where to hire virtual assistants, how to hire and train them, and what tasks you should outsource so that you too can move up the ladder to my definition of an entrepreneur.

But before we worry about what and how to outsource, we need to line up where to get our prospective virtual assistants. Let's get started.

Chapter 1: Why Virtual Assistants?

The Virtual World

It is no surprise that technology has changed the way our world works and how we interact. With the click of the mouse we are able to have instant gratification in all aspect of our lives and our businesses. Through all of this development, companies are increasingly looking to outsource tasks and functions within their business through the help of the "virtual world." This is why when you call your service provider or speak to a representative late in the day, you will usually get someone in another country reading a script to help answer all of your questions and solve your problems.

With that said, virtual assistants have been instrumental in helping businesses stay afloat in such a competitive market, and allowing a person to outsource themselves so they can focus on other, more involved aspects of their business. When you think of an eight-hour work day at a typical 9 – 5 job, how many hours are people actually working for the company versus the hours they are on the phone, in meetings, and completing random tasks? Studies have shown that in an eight-hour work day, most people actually work less than three to four hours on work-related items and end up wasting the rest of the time on irrelevant tasks. With the help of virtual assistants you can now focus eight hours on your business and train your VAs to focus on those random and menial tasks that need to get done in a given work day. More importantly, as you move towards hiring virtual assistants as employees, you can now monitor their work day, have them work only the three to four hours they are needed, and track their completion of tasks.

As the CEO of your business it is up to you to wear the entrepreneurial hat. If you are too bogged down in the repetitive tasks of your business, how can you make it grow? How can you track your efficiency in a system if you are the one who designed, created, is running, and managing it all at the same time? The answer is simple: you can't! It is important to get these tasks done which is where virtual assistants come into play. They help release you from those tedious tasks so you can focus on growth and building your business.

I still remember when I hired my first virtual assistant. I was trying to do it all. I was answering the phones, taking all the seller leads, running to meet private lenders, checking on every deal that came my way, doing the estimate reports, budgeting and maintaining the books, closing the deal, and still working a full time job. I realized that it was not only time to quit a job I didn't like, but it was also time to get help on some of these daunting tasks. Through my first virtual assistant, we were able to get two deals under contract in her first six weeks. We had her help us make offers on properties and run a few of our lead generation campaigns. This was crucial to our business as it freed up my time and allowed me to focus on other things like raising funds for the deal and finding new projects.

Moving forward, our virtual assistants have been able to help us by doing 75% of the tasks needed to be done within our business and, in one year of growth, we are now using them in all the different markets in which we invest. This has allowed us to close more deals due to their efficiency and consistency in the tasks they complete in a given day for us. I know if I can use virtual assistants to help me to scale my business in five different markets, you can too. I know it may seem easier said than done and I am constantly getting the questions: What was your background? How did you scale so quickly?

Well, it wasn't easy but I'm happy to let you see my background and my path to real estate success. I want you to see that the possibilities are truly endless and how you can achieve financial freedom much more quickly through the help of virtual assistants.

Chapter 2: My Story

What Inspired Me to Get Started?

While I was teaching long but rewarding hours in the Teach for America Program, I was given the book *Rich Dad, Poor Dad* by Robert Kiyosaki. I'm sure many of you have read it, but those who have not, go buy it NOW! What I appreciated so much about the book was the idea of determining your own worth and not letting someone else do it for you. In my business, I control how long and hard I want to work as well as how much I want to make. It all depends on my efforts and how effectively I train my team under me. The sooner I fire myself from each task, the faster I will climb up the ladder. I am also responsible for building my dream and worth and not someone else's.

Another message that also resonated with me is the idea that you don't have to be the sharpest tool in the shed to be successful. I know what my strengths are but I am more comfortable in telling you what my weaknesses are. In business, it is imperative that you know this about yourself so you can fill in the gaps accordingly. *Rich Dad, Poor Dad* allowed me to believe it was possible and while I am a professional student who loves to learn and will continue to take courses to improve my skills, you do not have to be at the top of your class to succeed in this business. You don't need a college or even a high school degree to be successful in this business. Your work ethic is the only thing that has to be 100% intact as that is what will distinguish you from your competition.

Surprisingly, teaching also taught me so much about how to be an effective business woman. I made sure my systems were extremely efficient in class, and each moment throughout the day students were working and their progress was being tracked. All these systems I learned and created as a teacher are also needed when running a business. I am constantly working on increasing efficiency within my system, making sure consistency happens in my business daily, and that I am constantly tracking and tweaking those systems. By doing that, I have been able to do over a dozen wholesale and rehab real estate investment deals in four different states.

My "Why"

I tell everyone the reason I believe people don't make it to the next level in business or accomplish all of their goals is sometimes because their "why" isn't strong enough. My "why" wakes me up early in the morning and makes me stay up late at night. My why is my mother and the desire to fulfill my purpose in life. I could write a whole book about my mom's influence in my life. She has worked for over 20 years as a school nurse and my why is to retire her. Buying my mother a house and retiring her so she can live out the remainder of her life in utter happiness is my motivation. Because my why is so strong, it allows me to set short term goals for myself and hold myself accountable for those goals. I wake up asking how I am getting closer to achieving my goals.

Your "why" doesn't have to be as personal as mine, but it better be strong enough to motivate you when times are tough and you feel like quitting. I've had tough days in business—everyone does—but I don't stop waking up each morning to have a better day than yesterday. I've seen too many people start this business and quit it because they were too afraid of failing. Your why should be strong enough to make you believe failure is not an option. Revisit your why often and make sure it is strong enough to help you not quit when times get tough.

It felt so good to be able to buy her the dream car she has always wanted in 2015 as a token of my appreciation for all that she has done for me. My next big project is to retire her in 2016 so she can relax, enjoy, and of course, help my business prosper.

How Have Virtual Assistants Helped Me Earn Multiple Streams of Income?

I feel this is important to note because I wasn't aware of how much money there is to be made in real estate. My friends have nicknamed me the "7 Streams Queen" because I am constantly thinking about different streams of income and ways to get paid from things that I do daily in my business. I would like to share these ways with you as I think it will be beneficial to see all the possibilities firsthand.

Stream one is my full time flipping business. My motto is "raise funds by the day and flip by night." My day is spent mostly talking with private moneylenders so that we can raise funds for our projects.

We are currently doing deals in four states: New Jersey, Maryland, Florida, and Ohio, as well as Washington, D.C. We are wholesaling, doing full rehab projects in these different areas, and accumulating rentals. Our virtual assistants play an active role in helping us find wholesale leads, manage the rehab projects, and accumulate rentals for us.

My second stream of income is investing my money, and helping my brothers, mom, and other family members and friends invest through self-directed IRAs in other people's real estate projects. I had a 403(b) from my previous employer as a teacher and when I worked for a university. I rolled both of them over when I became self-employed into a self-directed IRA that allowed me to invest money in different projects. I make sure that as an investor I am getting a minimum of a 12% return. I also push to get flat interest versus annual interest. My virtual assistants have been crucial in helping me select projects to put my family's money into as well as helping me with preparing all the documents that are needed for these transactions.

My third stream of income, which is my absolute favorite, is using my profit from my sources of income to buy rental properties. This is the biggest avenue of wealth money has to offer. Having rentals generates passive income that hits my account on a certain day of the month, every month, no matter where I am or what I am doing. My partner and I look to buy rentals all over as long as the return on investment (ROI) is sufficient and we have an excellent property manager/contractor in place to manage the rental. Now that we buy rentals quite often, we have also been fortunate to receive a finder's fee for helping other investors, family members, and friends who are looking to buy rentals in our areas to get an excellent ROI.

Our virtual assistants were crucial in creating a process that allows me to scout all the different rental leads, purchase them via auctions/motivated sellers, etc. and put renters in them ASAP. They also help with the property management aspect in making sure that our property manager has everything up to date for our renters and by scheduling times with our contractor to go check on the property for us and complete the repairs. They also manage the payment system of collections for a few of our properties.

One of our rental properties in Columbus, Ohio.

My fourth stream of income is using my real estate license to help a few clients sell their houses at retail price. Or even better, I use it to list the houses that we already bought and rehabbed on the market to get the commission added on to our profit. I also get paid as a Realtor, (which is my fifth stream of income) for referrals I provide through affiliate marketing. Funny enough, affiliate marketing could easily be its own six-figure business. When we refer painters, cabinet guys, contractors, etc., we get paid for referring business to them. (Exactly as we pay referrals to lenders, sellers, buyers and people who bring us deals. We can pay anywhere from $500 - $2,000 for a referral fee for a property.)

HOW DOES

AFFILIATE MARKETING

WORK?

AFFILIATE PUTS YOUR AD ON THEIR WEBSITE.

CUSTOMER CLICKS & CONVERTS.

CONVERSIONS ARE TRACKED

AFFILIATE GETS A COMMISSION, YOU GET A SALE!

My sixth stream of income is consulting with small businesses, which is probably my lowest-paying gig as I help a lot of people pro bono. I do try to help as many people as I can who are going through a tough situation or just need motivation to take their business to the next level! As a result I have created a consulting course to help real estate professionals leverage their time, money, and resources so that they can wear the entrepreneur hat rather than a technician one. This reference actually comes from the book I mentioned earlier, *The E-Myth Revisited*. It is the mentality and tactics of firing yourself and making your systems more efficient that Gerber discusses which absolutely made my business successful.

Speaking engagements are my seventh stream of income. Speaking allows me to share a large amount of information with students, aspiring business owners, and current entrepreneurs, helping to inspire people to establish and grow their businesses.

Chapter 3: What Will Be Your Virtual Plan?

Read NO Further if You Are a Person Who Reads but NEVER Takes Action!

Information Without Action is Worthless

This topic is clearly a pet peeve of mine so I decided to make a small section about it because I must address it. I have probably spoken to hundreds of people who have called me about my business to ask how we invest in four different states or have virtual assistants scaling up our business to the next level. I have literally only met two people who have actually taken what I said and put it into action.

I had a unique conversation with a woman at an investor meeting a few months back and told her how there was a genuine investor in Baltimore who has a website filled with free information that contains all the information I paid a company to receive. I told her he should be worried about giving away all that information as I've already started to implement his systems and tweaked it to my market. I said if the right person gets his information and really starts doing his systems in his own market, he would have some heavy competition. She looked at me and started laughing hysterically.

She said, "Sweet Brittney, you are not the average person who attends a free workshop. In a room full of fifty people that heard his exact presentation with you, probably about 25 people actually wrote down accurately the systems he is using, from that pool about 15 people researched one or two of the tools he mentioned, from there seven people actually created free accounts with the tools, three people from that pool went and took the time to train themselves on the tools and maybe implemented one thing partially that he mentioned and only one person named Brittney Calloway actually replicated and scaled his entire virtual system."

Her words stunned me as it really hit me that more than 85% of people who buy into real estate courses, books, coaching, etc., do not go through with the systems or the program that was given to them. I have been guilty of this in the past but no more! For every workshop or seminar I attend, I try to implement at least three of the strategies I heard in my business.

It is easy to lose momentum if we get bogged down in too many tasks and it causes us to slow down completely and let our projects taper off. This is why it is important to outsource a lot of these tasks so we can implement new things in our businesses to help them grow.

Getting Things DONE

I consider myself to be an action taker but when this woman said those words to me I realized one of my key strengths is follow up. On Mondays I literally map out everything I have to do, just like the old school to-do list format. What separates me from others is that I don't allow many things to be put off until next week, which will keep on getting pushed to the next week, and then will eventually fall off the list.

Instead, I make a point to complete things on my to-do list in a matter of two weeks. We all have been there. However, I make a serious effort to work on each action item daily, even if it is for 30 minutes. As long as progress was made it still can remain an action item and will get done within a reasonable amount of time.

I also was NEVER a morning person; I swear I almost failed a 9:30 am yoga class in college because I was consistently late. However, I wake up now at 6:00 am religiously. I get the bulk of my action items done, which allows me to feel productive before my day has even started. A real estate agent told me that he works hard core, non-stop until 12 noon because once lunch hits everything after that is done with half production. That has been my constant struggle. My morning classes as a teacher were always more rigorous and productive as opposed to my afternoon classes.

When I worked for a university, I would complete way more projects when I came in early in the morning versus the afternoon when the phone is ringing and more people call and things just fall by the wayside. That is my personal system. I know people who are the most productive during the night and work from 8:00 pm until 1:30 am and accomplish all their tasks. Do what works for you, but the first step is to accurately know what works for you and be consistent with the schedule you set for yourself. I say all this to say, now is the time to consider yourself the one who is going to implement everything that I further write in this book. You can't implement everything tomorrow, but day by day you keep working on it and you too will have a million dollar business, as you will learn to outsource your most tedious administrative tasks so you can focus on entrepreneurial tasks.

How Have I Stayed in Business? How Will You Stay in Business?

The answer is quite simple: Systems, Systems, and more Systems! When you have systems you are able to create consistency. When you have consistency you are able to increase your productivity. At one time, my virtual assistant could only submit seven offers in an hour and now she is up to fifteen. Once you increase your productivity you are then able to increase your revenue and then hire more employees. When you are able to hire more employees you are able to leverage your Time and Time isn't just money: it is EVERYTHING! We leverage our time by using virtual assistants.

The key is to scale up as quickly as possible. The easiest way to start doing that is to document every aspect of your business as if a fifth grader were reading your manual and trying to figure out how to do each step. When cleaning out our house, I found an old book report a teacher once asked our class to do. She gave me A on it and literally wrote:

"Way to follow directions."

Looking back at the directions I thought to myself how could anyone possibly get lower than a B on this as she told us step-by-step what to do.

Literally the directions read: "Step 1: Place your name, title of your paper, and date in 12 pt font using Times Roman font in the middle of the page." This was worth 5 points. I'm sure someone didn't follow directions and lost some points.

The point is to show—step-by-step—what you want so that when it comes time to hire virtual assistants they know exactly what the expectation is and it cannot be debated. Once you document your business in a manual as I have, anyone can be trained on it. If one of our virtual assistants were to quit tomorrow, we could easily hire a new one and in a few days have our systems back up and running so that nothing goes undone.

The next step is being consistent; I have touched on this a little bit. Our schedule is set for our virtual assistants every hour that they are designated to work. They know exactly what their tasks are and the beauty is that while we are asleep, they are wide awake and working on getting things done for our business. It is true that our business is being worked on 24 hours a day by someone. Every day, at the top of the morning, one of our virtual assistants is putting offers on properties, the next hour is cold calling, the next is auction scouting or social media, etc. The tasks vary by day but it is a consistent schedule that she is to follow each week. Her day is outlined from 9:00 am to 5:00 pm and she has something to do every hour. She is consistent in what she does daily and always has a project to work on.

We do the same thing as a team to hold ourselves accountable. Every Wednesday at our team meeting, there is a check-in for all team members to show their numbers for what they accomplished the past week, accounting for each hour they were given a task. We even have friendly competitions where the lowest performer has to do something for everyone else and the highest performer gets a reward for the week. Everyone on the team is responsible to report their wins and losses and everyone walks away with a set of tasks to do.

A key million dollar business trend I have come across is that every performing business has weekly check-ins and team meetings. Setting aside this time every week in your business will allow you to grow exponentially in productivity. It allows you to reflect on what is working and what isn't, track numbers on tasks being performed, and tweak or create new systems. This is key to productivity and I recommend all businesses create this weekly accountability piece in order to be successful.

In addition to our weekly meetings, we have benchmarked goals that we aim for each quarter. This allows our team to stay focused on why these daily tasks must be performed and how they are important to our overall company goals and the benchmarks that we are trying to hit. We also are constantly trying to scale up by firing ourselves from a position and outsourcing it to someone else. We continue to monitor how we, as partners in business together, are working to fire ourselves from different roles so that we can once again leverage our time to do other things.

My Routine

I put this in here as many of the clients I coached said that they became more productive when they followed my actual morning routine. If you have one already that you do and your productivity levels are where you need them to be, then keep it and use these as suggestions to help you along the way.

Your morning routine should be customized for you but the days where my morning routine is spot on, my productivity levels have been the highest in completing the tasks on my to-do list for the day. I literally find myself waking up at 6:00 am and finishing everything by 2:00 pm so that I can take random calls and thoroughly enjoy the rest of my day. However, nothing after 2:00 pm is really work-related or something pertinent that needs to get done. Things tend to fall by the wayside when my morning routine is not done and causes me to play catch up all day.

The first thing that I do when I wake up is listen to an inspirational podcast to start my day. My mindset is very important to how I complete my day. If I have too much on my mind or am worried about the day, I won't complete a lot of the tasks. Listening to an inspirational podcast is extremely helpful as it sets a positive mindset and takes away all the stress in completing my to-do list.

After the podcast, I do 30 to 45 minutes of exercise. Sometimes I run to clear my mind but most days I do a high intensity exercise routine for 30 minutes. This helps me to not be sluggish later in the day.

I then make a healthy breakfast or a shake and review my vision board that has all my goals and things I want to accomplish for the next year and my to-do list for the day. This is all done before 7:00 am when everyone wakes up.

Every time I do my morning routine, I feel great and accomplish so much. Testimonials from others show the same results. Some people vary by going to the gym or doing a workout series like Insanity or Jillian Michaels. Customize it to your benefit but it is important to listen to something inspirational, exercise, and review your goals before the day starts. If you can't fit it all into your morning routine, I would at least suggest listening to something inspirational and reviewing your goals.

They say only 10% of people today actually write down their goals and look at them every day. Those who do are 100% more likely to accomplish them in a reasonable time versus people who don't write out or have their goals posted anywhere. By looking at these goals and visualizing your success, you will accomplish them.

My Mindset in Business—What Will Yours Be?

My life, my why, my motto, and routine that I included earlier are so important to add to this book. I hope you enjoyed it as I think it is important for you to understand why I have become so successful. In addition to my routine, my mindset is equally important. I must include it because it is easy to say, "Go read this book and teach your virtual assistants what I taught mine and you will be successful," but that isn't entirely true. If you don't know how I operate on a daily basis or the mindset that I have, how will you truly be successful? I'm passionate about making sure you have all the pieces needed to see this thing through and be successful.

There is an important mindset that I think I have that many don't have, which has allowed me to be successful in training virtual assistants and getting people to work with me for such a long time. You have to understand that you are not in the business of making money; you are truly in the business of helping people. Every person I have ever taken the time to help has brought me ten more positive outcomes to my business that I could not have received had I not taken the time to initially help them. When you take the time to truly help people—not so you can come out on top with the biggest bucks—but really help someone to learn systems, learn financial independence, or help change the trajectory of someone's life, all parties win.

Money is a motivator to do more deals but the thought should never be how can I screw someone over so that I can make more cash. We are extremely generous in how we train people because the goal is not to have an assistant stuck with us for ten years doing the same thing. We would love to turn that person into an acquisitions manager, later a project manager, and who knows, maybe even a partner. The idea is that you want to ask your employees what their goals are and what they need to reach the next level in their development so you can make sure you are constantly meeting their needs. Also, when you train and help people in your business you are without a doubt sharpening your skills and able to develop tweaks in systems or think of ideas to increase the effectiveness in what you already have in place. This is without a doubt an important mindset to elevating your business.

Communication is key with everything we do, so it is absolutely essential that we communicate with our virtual assistants and interns regularly and effectively. The question I ask people in order to see where they stand on having a mindset like me is: If a project with no guidelines or structure isn't completed the way you wanted it to be done... whose fault is it?

I have to let that sink in because the answer should be that it is always your fault. Every time a task is not done to my liking, I am constantly thinking what did I not say or communicate for it to turn out the way it did. Now there will be some people who after six or seven tries at explaining a task still won't get it right. Those people, yes, we should let go. However, most of us get to Try Number Two and are fuming and ready to fire the person we have working for us but in truth, we gave no guidelines to begin with. This is why documentation and communication are important.

When we document our system and take the time to show people how we want things done, we will get perfect results. I allow for mistakes to occur a few times in the beginning but am positive in my feedback and always complimenting what my assistants did well before I criticize what mistakes they need to work on! I am also notorious for giving surprise little bonuses for when tasks are completed early or done to perfection! This makes people excited and motivated to work harder. Now that you understand my mindset, business model, and structure a little bit more, I want to "dive into the weeds" of how we pick someone to work for our company.

Our company motto is crucial to how we do business. For example, it is important to note is that we really do make sure our clients who are in foreclosure or pre-foreclosure are educated on all of their options and what the foreclosure process looks like. As soon as they type their information into our database, we send them a series of seven articles on the foreclosure process so they can look at all of the resources that are available to them through our company and resources in the area they are in. If I haven't said it once already I will say it again: our business is truly based on the model of helping people first.

Even if customers do not choose to work with our company, we still want to make sure they have the information on foreclosures, as it is important to know how the process works and what their options are. The same applies for probates, absentee owners, tax liens and extremely distressed properties. We have also had clients not use us to buy their house but have inquired about our credit repair service or our debt free program. If we are purchasing the house from our clients we will actually pay for the service for them, which many companies do not do. However, whether we get their business or not we are always willing to provide helpful services to them.

My Actual Deals Found Via Virtual Assistants

Our virtual team has truly taken our business to the next level. I will mention one of the deals we have gotten from our virtual team so that you can see the profits and success.

This deal was found through the MLS. Our virtual assistant on average makes about 50 offers a week on the MLS and this one was accepted. It was negotiated by my partner and he closed on it in a few weeks. This cost us about $25.00 in labor as that is what we pay the VA weekly to do our MLS offers.

The breakdown was buying it for $62,000, repairs were $50,000 and the sold price was $199,000. I'll let you do the math on the ROI. There are many more success stories and testimonials from people who I have worked with to build their virtual team who can testify to this system.

Now that you have read all about me, my inspiration to get started, my why, my mindset, and my success, let's dive into the weeds of how to build your virtual team and get your business generating six figures.

Chapter 4: Who Should Be On Your Team?

Virtual Assistant vs. Intern?

There is a difference between hiring a Virtual Assistant or an intern to help you run your business. Virtual Assistants do any and all tasks without being in the office or in a physical location. Our Virtual Assistants currently reside in the Philippines, India, and some parts of the U.S. There are many companies that advertise virtual assistants; they usually tend to fall into two categories: trained in general or specific *skills* (like graphic design) or trained in specific *businesses* like real estate.

There are companies that facilitate hiring virtual assistants who have no training in real estate or your business, but have some experience in particular areas that you may need them for (i.e., social marketing or web design). They typically are lower in cost but require more work on the front end, as you have to train them on your real estate systems in order to see efficiency and productivity. For example, we have had great experience finding coachable virtual assistants off Upwork (formerly known as Odesk). They weren't trained in real estate but came with some knowledge in marketing, Excel, number crunching, etc. However, we had to do the leg work and take the time to show them how to navigate the real estate content that was applicable to our business.

In this category of cheaper virtual assistants who have basic knowledge on aspects of your business, there are also assistants that are great for specific projects and allow you to negotiate the project for a fee (i.e., designing a website). Fiverr.com or Elance/Upwork is great for designing business cards, logos, and websites. The project can be negotiated for a flat fee. The hard part is making sure you provide enough instructions for what you want upfront and/or knowing enough about the inner workings of a project like web design to be able to verbalize what you will like and won't like.

This way you and the virtual assistant working for you will not be frustrated by constant revisions. Also, as the gurus say, it is always better to have a project done imperfectly than perfect but not done. Sure, I could have gone back and forth a few more times on the logo to get it exactly the way I wanted it, but I got tired and in the interest of time said, "Let's go with this version. Get it on the website, cards, decals, stickers, letters, etc. so that it doesn't hinder my production in other areas." You never want to spend so much time on an aspect that is hindering you from doing business. Get the task completed and move on to more important things. Done is better than perfect!

The second category of virtual assistants—those that come partially trained in real estate and other business skills—are hired through companies on a longer term, regular schedule, for instance, 20 hours a week. You still have to train them to your system (i.e., making offers on the MLS in your city) but they do come trained with some knowledge of contracts and/or market research.

We have a virtual assistant who came to us real estate trained. She does marketing, makes offers, and helps us to manage our rehabs across the different states. We still had to show her our systems but the training time was much shorter as she was accustomed to real estate terms. This option is a bit more expensive but if you really don't have the time to train someone extensively it may be the best option.

Interns are a little different. They are typically in the office doing lower grade tasks to help enhance your business. They come in "seasons," based on school semesters, which is why your training manuals need to be on point so when one leaves you can easily train another. Interns can come from all different education levels and still add value to your business. My first intern was a freshman in high school who was part of a work-study school program. She worked in the office every Wednesday for free and did the social media aspect of our business, which she loved. She was also responsible for watching webinars that we didn't have time to watch and presenting a summary of the content to our team leaders along with suggestions and strategies that we should be trying.

There are also higher-level interns that we hired to do our marketing campaigns, who were college students working for the summer. Typically we contact different community colleges or college career development centers in order to post our job or go to career fairs to get the word out about our company. You can also attend career expos that people or companies are having so that you can promote your business and what you are working on to these students. You can call local high schools to post the job descriptions as well.

I called my alma mater and they were more than happy to help assist in getting me an intern for the summer. Also, the school sometimes has funding to support a student in their moving costs or living expenses so that you are really only paying the hourly fee, which worked well for us! This intern was responsible for creating marketing materials, adding buyers and sellers to our lists, as well as tracking leads, completing follow up calls, and making cold calls.

Now that you have some ideas on where to find these virtual assistants and interns, we can dive into the methods of training them.

Chapter 5: How Do You Build Your Team?

We put a lot of time into vetting our virtual assistants. We do so by making sure we first advertise to over 100 people about our job post. Through Monster, Indeed, Craigslist, and other sources, we make sure to post the position for all to take a look. Here is a sample ad that we have used to retain a virtual assistant:

REAL ESTATE VIRTUAL ASSISTANT WANTED

Real Estate Company needs someone to work virtually 10 to 15 hours a week taking incoming phone calls from buyers and sellers. We are looking for someone reliable who has some flexibility in their schedule as these calls can come in at all times during the day. For every deal that closes on a call made via our assistant, they will receive a cash bonus. In addition, we are looking for someone who we can train into a higher position such as a project manager, acquisition manager, and maybe even a partner. Customer service or sales experience is preferred. You must feel comfortable on the phone talking with people.

Job Description:

- Take 3 to 10 incoming calls a day from buyers, sellers, and tenants and set appointments.

- You will be filling out scripts and entering leads into a database.

- You will have to then run CMAs – Competitive Market Analysis -- on the property to enter into the database as well. (We will show you how.)

- You will also be doing online marketing to generate additional real estate leads from posting ads on Craigslist, to searching the MLS, to more advanced online lead generation efforts.

- Other marketing projects may be given to you as well.

- Hours may increase depending on business and computer skills.

- Online marketing experience a definite plus.

Pay & Requirements:
- $6 per hour

- You will be paid as a sub-contractor and will bill me according to time spent

- Basic Microsoft Office skills are needed

- Basic Internet skills needed

- Start immediately

If interested, please email your resume to (Your Name Here) at (Your Email Address Here)

- Compensation: $6

- Principals only. Recruiters please don't contact this job poster.

- Please, no phone calls about this job!

- Please do not contact job poster about other services, products or commercial interests.

I've had a few people reach out to me saying they tried posting ads but that no one responded. My first question is always "Was the post compelling and if you saw it would you apply for it?" When it comes to posts, now is not the time to be lazy. My advice when advertising would be to pick a post that is energetic and grabs people's attention. You have to go back and remember what grabbed you to your 9 - 5 jobs, if you can think back that far. Was it the post, benefits, career goals? What exactly are you offering that makes it compelling to work at your company? Go on Craigslist yourself and look at interesting posts for the job that you want a virtual assistant to do so you can see the competition you have from different companies.

You want to make sure your post is geared towards a wide range of people and captures the attention of potential virtual assistants who will be working in your company. I'd like to point out a couple of things in our ad that have always attracted our virtual assistants.

The first point is we specifically make sure we let people know the potential growth they can have in our company. Many of us in our 9 – 5 jobs become stuck in a position once we realize there really is nowhere to go but to be the boss of the company or to apply to other companies in order to move up. Here in this ad, we are very specific and mention the opportunity for growth on purpose as we would much rather have one assistant that has been with us for a long time and who we can continue to promote versus someone who wants to go from job to job.

Another thing to highlight is our bonus system, which is what I think truly does keep our virtual assistants on our team. $6.00 an hour isn't the highest paid job out there and we recognize that. However, once we close on a deal that our virtual assistant helped us find, we do make sure that we pay our assistants a bonus for finding it. What is $500 - $1,000 off a $20,000 profit? When you pay your people well, you keep them motivated and hungry for more. We make sure that we do this so that we keep our team happy.

We put a preliminary "test" in the ad by asking for a cover letter along with the resume. We ask for a cover letter not for the sole purpose of reading it but so we could see which applicants will actually take the time to complete the task. We want people who want to work for us and who will complete every task we ask of them with 100% accuracy. The cover letter also allows us to assess their level of English language proficiency, as well as communication skills.

I personally don't get too critical about what the cover letter says; we do this more so we can weed out the people who neglected to write one to begin with. It is easy to send your resume to 100 jobs without even looking at what they are. This technique allows us to see who really does have an interest in our specific job and who wants to be a part of our company.

These are just some tips to keep in mind as you start to create job posts for your virtual assistants. The key thing to remember is making sure you advertise growth, showing them the opportunity for bonuses and ways to create additional streams of income. You also want to have a small test in the application to make sure people follow directions. Maybe it is a cover letter or maybe it's a format in which the resume should be delivered.

You want to make sure that test is in there as you will notice the applicants who will not follow your one simple direction. If they can't follow that then what is to say that they will follow other simple directions? Once you have received a plethora of resumes and cover letters from different applicants, it is time to weed them out a little bit more through an interview.

How Do You Interview Them?

A good interview takes roughly 30 to 45 minutes to complete. It is important to make sure that they think the company is a right fit for them and more importantly, you think they are a right fit for you.

The first step should be to make sure there is a thorough introduction about yourself and the company, as well as your goals and what you are trying to accomplish this year, and how this position specifically will help you attain your goals.

The next step should be to review with the candidate their goals and how they think they can add value to the company. I also think it is important to ask what the virtual assistant's career goals are. You want to make sure that you, the company, and the position will actually develop your virtual assistant in the way that they want to be developed and that they are reaching their benchmarked goals. I have also included some samples of more specific interview questions so that you can really determine who will be the best person for the job:

1. **What experience do you have in the following areas <use your task list for specifics>:** *It is important to make sure that your VA is comfortable with the tasks you want them to do. Remember though, training can always be done through the manual you will have that documents all of your systems.*

2. **What are your hours of operation?** *Make sure you understand where your VA is located and that they understand that your deadlines are based on your time zone.*

3. **What is your work experience?** *While a very traditional question, you want to see if their skills are conducive to what you're doing. Plus, it's a good relationship builder. It also doesn't hurt to ask them about work experience that is specific to the tasks that you want them to complete.*

4. **What are your strengths? What do you struggle with?** *Think about your needs and whether you can work with someone who may struggle with a key area you need help with.*

5. **What is your preferred form of communication?** *When working with someone online or virtually, it is essential that you understand how they want to work and receive communication. It could be email, Skype, video, etc. You also want to make sure that they understand the communication standards if you are having them do calls or send emails.*

6. **Are you willing to sign a non-disclosure agreement?** *This isn't a deal-killer, but it could be for some people. If you have great strategies, you don't want them to be shared with everyone. Best to keep business secrets and training manual login information protected by the disclosure agreement.*

7. **After hearing about my business and technologies used, what questions do you have?** *A good virtual assistant will listen, take notes, and have something to ask.*

8. **Are you still interested in working for me now that you know more about what I do and what I'm looking for?** *Look out for hesitation.*

General Questions

Tell me about yourself.

_____

_____

_____

_____

What interests you about this particular job?

_____

_____

_____

_____

What would you say is the most important thing you are looking for in a job?

_____

_____

What is your timeline to begin working?

_____

_____

Work History

What was your working environment like at your previous job?

_____
_____
_____
_____

What type of responsibilities did you enjoy at your previous job?

_____
_____
_____
_____

How would your previous boss comment on your overall performance?

_____
_____
_____
_____
_____

Do you have a written referral from your previous employer?

_____
_____
_____

May we call? _____

Speak with whom?

_____

Phone_____

Describe Your Previous Boss/Like Dislike?

_____
_____

What did you dislike about your previous job?

_____

_____

What were your work hours like?

_____

_____

Did you like them? _____

How much did you get paid?

_____

_____

Strengths & Weaknesses

Everyone has strengths and weaknesses. Tell me what you are best at.

_____

_____

_____

_____

What are your weaknesses?

_____

_____

_____

_____

Have you ever failed at something in your professional career?

_____

_____

_____

_____

*Tell me of a time you took a risk and failed.

_____

_____

_____

_____

Motivation

What motivates you?

_____

_____

_____

_____

What is it that interests you about this job?

_____

_____

_____

_____

What are your goals for this job?

_____

_____

_____

_____

Where do you see yourself 5 years from now?

_____

_____

_____

_____

Assistant Questions

Has anyone in your family started their own business?

_____

_____

Have you worked in an entrepreneurial environment?

_____

_____

How savvy are you with Outlook from 1 to 10?

_____

_____

Have you ever answered email for someone before?

_____

_____

If so, how did you organize it?

_____

_____

_____

How savvy are you with Excel from 1 to 10?

_____

_____

Have you done bookkeeping or accounting before – 1 to 10?

_____

_____

Have you worked in retail or customer service before?

_____

_____

Are you more of a sales person or an organizational person?

_____

_____

Have you worked in sales before?

_____

_____

Please rate your organizational skills and give a valid example of them.

_____

_____

_____

_____

Please rate your sales skills and give a valid example of them.

_____

_____

_____

_____

What interests you about being a personal assistant?

_____

_____

_____

_____

What do you think the role of a personal assistant should be?

_____

_____

_____

_____

Are there any tasks you have not enjoyed performing as a personal assistant before and why?

_____

_____

_____

_____

Give me an example of how a personal assistant can help someone.

_____

_____

_____

Does selling real estate interest you?

_____

_____

_____

_____

Do you have any experience processing RE transactions?

_____

_____

_____

_____

Are you a multi-tasker or do you prefer to focus and why?

_____

_____

_____

_____

How do you stay focused?

_____

_____

_____

_____

Give an example of how you multi-task.

_____

_____

_____

Give an example of a project you recently completed from start to finish and how you stayed on track.

_____

_____

_____

Would you rather create business systems or follow them?

_____

_____

_____

Give an example of when you created a business system.

_____

_____

_____

_____

These are just a few sample questions but these are all very crucial questions to make sure you weed out the people who are not qualified or able to complete the tasks needed. The phone interview is to really test for communication skills, people skills, as well as problem solving skills. The candidates we picked for the final interview were personable which enabled us to use them to answer phone calls and emails. We also looked for people who were able to answer real life problem solving scenarios with poise and compassion.

Next we will move onto how to make sure you pick the best people for your team.

How Do You Pick the Best Candidates to Hire?

The old saying goes, you can lead a horse to water but you can't make it drink. It's the same when approaching virtual assistants. You can provide the opportunity to everyone, but you can't make it the best fit for everyone. When we advertised the virtual assistant job, we advertised on all possible outlets such as Craigslist, Upwork (formerly Odesk and Elance), Monster, Indeed, international career websites, and virtual hiring fairs, as mentioned previously.

We had a few people initially apply who fit the depth of experience that we wanted. However, some were extremely slow to set up a time for the interview and overall became too busy to finish the final steps of our interview process. We even hired one who was great in her field for MLS offers but quit after two weeks because she found something better.

Therefore, it became apparent that we should give interviews to the people who really wanted the job and contacted us to follow up on the status of their application. Even if they had less experience, we weren't hesitant to bring them on the team because our training materials could be given to a high school student and anyone with that level of education could do the job.

We also picked people who had a willingness to learn. If we had picked someone at the top of their field with social media or web design, prices would have been hard to negotiate. When we picked team players who had enough skill but wanted to learn more and were willing to be dedicated to our company and grow with us, we had more success. In addition, the final test for each skill set really did help us determine who was going to be a good fit.

We give tests such as create a Craigslist post from the manual and then add two things that we tell them that are not in the manual to assess their skills. We try to see how good they are at following things step-by-step in addition to how well they can listen to steps that were not fully written down for them. This lets us know how much work we can give them without having to monitor them.

How Do You Pay Them?

There are many ways to pay virtual assistants for their services. We pay them in various ways, depending on the job they are doing: for the completion of a project, for miscellaneous tasks, as well as by the hour. For example, one of our virtual assistants is paid for how many offers she submits, not how many hours she works on submitting offers. There is a huge difference. There are big bonuses if she hits a certain amount of offers in a week and, if we get a house under contract and then sell it, she gets paid a hefty bonus. But by paying per offers submitted versus an hourly rate, we cut our costs significantly in any given week.

We also pay small amounts for tasks such as $5.00 for a newsletter that goes out to our lenders every week so they can see what projects we are working on. We really only like to pay by the hour for demanding tasks, i.e., cold calling Realtors, sellers, attorneys, or managing a rehab. These are larger tasks that require a higher level of skill set which is why we typically will pay an hourly rate.

The key is to always give incentives or bonuses when your assistants go above and beyond. When you keep them happy they will keep you happy. I am also a key advocate for giving small raises every six months. Even if it is small (i.e., instead of getting $3.93 for 10 offers we will give you $4.00 for 10 offers), it allows people to see progression and feel like they are reaching new heights.

Chapter 6: How to Train and Evaluate Your Team

How to Train Virtual Assistants

In my former job as a Special Education Teacher, the method of choice to teaching a lesson that would be retained was through the "I do, We do, You do" method. I learned this when I was a part of the Teach for America program. Such a simple concept that applies to so many things I do in my daily life now! It's especially useful in how I train and teach my virtual assistants and interns.

As they say, once a teacher always a teacher. Typically, I would show my students different ways to master a task. I would demonstrate how to do it first, we would then walk through it together, and then I would have them do the task all by themselves a few times to ensure they had mastered the skill. My last step was to have them complete a short exit assessment to make sure they retained the information and would be ready to demonstrate mastery in the next class.

This method is exactly what I do in training my virtual assistants. I have my manual, which, as I mentioned earlier, documents my entire business. I walk my assistants step-by-step through a task in the manual and show it to them on my screen. I then have us do it together while I ask a few comprehension questions to make sure they understand. Next, they show me how to do it on their own. I then have them do a quick assessment of the concept in the manual so they can demonstrate that they did do it correctly. This is very important so we can troubleshoot any questions they have.

Remember when documenting your business: no step is too menial and more description is always better than less. I.e., for documenting how to post on Facebook, the first step would be open a new browser and go to Facebook.com. Every key stroke, every research tactic should be documented so that even a high school student can figure out how to complete the steps to running my business. It is important to never give a task randomly and have expectations in your head that you did not convey. This is always a recipe for disaster.

You cannot expect people to read your mind or to complete tasks when you haven't explained them in detail. Writing a manual for your business is a lot of work, but it is better to do more work on the front end and document everything so that these virtual assistants can know your exact expectations for the task at hand, rather than trying to gauge it through a short email conversation or quick calls when things go sour.

By doing this, I have increased efficiency in our business and other clients' businesses by over 30% in production. These tasks that you take time to document turn into routines, which turn into systems that you can build upon. We all know that systems are key to being able to reach your dreams of sipping margaritas on the beach while you close a deal in your real estate business. When you truly start to outsource your business and put systems in place, you can then move up the ladder to focus on the more important hat—the entrepreneur hat—that allows you to decide where and how to take your business to the next level.

How to Evaluate VAs and Interns

You should, without a doubt, have an example for every task that you are assigning. This allows you to point out mistakes using constructive criticism so they know exactly where they made an error. I also think it is extremely important to have weekly meetings with your virtual assistants to discuss progress and any improvements that are needed to the system. In addition, it is important to discuss their overall growth and how they are contributing to the company as well as asking what other skills they want to learn that will take them to the next level.

This is not like a performance review, which was my least favorite thing to do when I worked for a university. I hated it because my boss would literally tell me I was doing fine but then never explained why I couldn't get a raise. Always explain to people why they are doing the task they are doing and how they are vital to your company. When you explain that to them and allow them to see their value, they will rise to the occasion and exceed your expectations. If they do go above and beyond, be affirming in your words to help motivate them to get to the next level.

Our Business Model

One thing I must highlight in our business model is what we do that really separates us from other investors. Not only are we willing to help our customers by buying their house, we are willing to scrub their credit and have them work with a credit specialist so that they are able to move forward from this situation and be set up for financial success in the next few years. In addition, we are also willing to pay for moving costs so that they don't have to worry about getting into further financial hardship.

We offer debt free counseling so they are able to work with a specialist who will teach them financial literacy and investments. Our hope is that they are able to learn and pass on this education about financial independence to their children. Another popular service that we will do (on occasion if the numbers work and clients agree) is to put aside a small investment account for them so that we can build an ongoing relationship and they can become our private money lenders on different projects. That way we are helping our sellers grow their money and they can turn around and work with us now as a private lender.

Once again, the goal isn't to make the biggest profit off our clients but to truly help and change the trajectory of our clients' lives. Not everyone will want each service and others will take advantage of all of them. Again, this is truly a matter of whatever will fit our clients' most pressing needs. I have also included a snap shot of our business model so you can see exactly how our systems operate and how we have been able to scale so quickly.

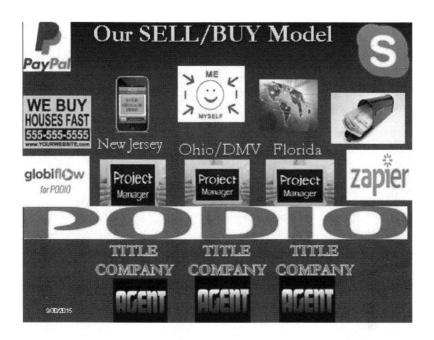

While I will dive into the weeds more on each specific tool, this is a great snapshot of how everything works in our business. As you can see, I'm at the top of the model. I personally am monitoring all of the campaigns that we have. We have our bandit sign campaign that is used to funnel in leads. We also have a text messaging and voicemail system that allows us to reach out to sellers in our market to bring them in as leads.

We use direct mail campaigns as well as internet marketing campaigns to bring in leads. All of these leads are coming in via the web or people calling our business number, which are both run by our virtual assistants. Our VAs handle all the calls that come to our business line. They take down all the information, and put the leads into Podio, our free database which holds all of our leads. (Podio is a great marketing tool that works with lists, systems, and follow-up campaigns.) They also are responsible for running the numbers and making offers for all the leads that look credible and fit our buying criteria.

From there, my partner or I will review the offers to see if there are good leads that we should absolutely call the next day, ones that we can submit to our Realtor to put in the offer, or ones that we will follow up on once the price goes down. If we put in offers that aren't accepted, we have them on a timeline to follow up with them in a few weeks.

Once the offers are accepted, we then go and have our contractors look at the property, raise the funds, and go to closing. If we are wholesaling it we have our VAs get our wholesaling package and checklist together. Once we know that we are going to close on a property, we and our VAs get the paperwork ready and submit it all to the title company so we can go to closing. We just wash, rinse, and repeat this process for every deal that comes our way.

We use Skype to communicate with our VAs and we use PayPal to pay them for their work. GlobiFlow and Zapier are tools that are used in Podio to help us host all the different marketing campaigns we are doing in our business. In Podio, you can run your autoresponder campaign for your leads that came to you, but didn't work out in the beginning. You can also use it to send a newsletter to your lenders. GlobiFlow and Zapier also aid in those processes as well.

Now that you have seen our business model, let's dive into all the ways we use our virtual assistants and how they have made our business grow.

Chapter 7: The Weeds of What VAs Can Do

What Your Virtual Assistant Can Do

There are a few aspects of your real estate business that if you outsource to virtual assistants or interns, your business production will absolutely increase at a level of 30% or higher so that you can focus on wearing the entrepreneur hat and scaling your business to the next level. Your virtual assistants can help with social media marketing, accounting, direct marketing, managing of calendars, generating leads, and anything else you consider to be menial or repetitive tasks.

This is critical to running your business. These virtual assistants who you hire should have excellent English speaking and writing capabilities to communicate with your customers. While each task given is spelled out in our manual for admin responsibilities, many concepts and protocols must be taught that are customized and tailored to our business.

A very easy way to manage your time is when you have a virtual assistant managing your calendar. When calls come in it is important for a virtual assistant to be aware of what is spam so that you are not wasting your time talking to telemarketers. Virtual assistants can take calls and make calls to schedule appointments for you with motivated sellers, private lenders, contractors, Realtors and any other major business partners. They can also keep track of action items, deadlines, messages, and relevant business issues, both internal and external. Once you are able to explain who should be on your calendar versus someone who is not really adding value to your business, they can use their better judgment when trying to arrange and rearrange your calendar.

By working with your VA daily, you will be able to teach your virtual assistants how to make appropriate, informed decisions regarding your available time. Once the key players in your business are identified, the assistant will be able to prioritize your contacts to ensure your days are successful and not a lot of time is being wasted.

Just as they can screen incoming calls, they can also do this for email correspondence. Rather than you reading those 300+ emails a day, they can determine the priority and respond appropriately. They can also alert you and make recommendations as needed regarding appropriate action and follow-up for individuals who contact you. They can do the preliminary research on the 100 leads you get via email and alert you if any are worth following up on.

If you do not have an assistant answering the phone for you 24/7 (and you should as there are companies that will do that for you), you can have your virtual assistants gather voicemail and phone messages and send them to you. They can also be trained to reach back out to each person who called as well as take initiative on deciding the appropriate actions or resources for each message received.

When you have to attend conferences, workshops, or (my favorite) travel on vacation, you can have your virtual assistant make travel arrangements as needed and put together your itinerary for the trip. They can also be extremely helpful in creating, editing, and formatting documents such as letters of thanks or newsletters. In addition, they can be a major help with direct mail, marketing materials, Excel spreadsheets, PowerPoints, and other related documents for your business. They can also be of assistance in tracking the progress of your documents that need to be signed, like a contract, a mortgage, deed, or promissory note as well as helping to file documents in folders to keep track of different contracts or files related to a flip, which can later also be helpful when it comes to filing taxes.

Overall, they are helpful in ensuring a smooth system for sellers, buyers, contact database management, and back office support. My favorite is their ability to help with the stages of the rehab as a virtual project manager. From putting in the offer, to scheduling contractors to meet on the site to give updates, to coordinating payment schedules, to coordinating pictures for the weekly newsletter, listing the property, scheduling the staging and aiding with the showing feedback, and closing, you are really able to duplicate yourself and have a virtual assistant track the stages of your rehab or even a listing.

If you are like me and have your real estate license, the possibilities are also endless as to what a virtual assistant can help you do to maximize your real estate business. They can set up showings, listings, open houses, and help you put your entire real estate agent business on autopilot. They can coordinate all the inspections with owners and keep them regularly informed on the stages of the selling process. They can add your stack of business card contacts to a database, run queries, export data, maintain listings and closings, referrals, create/update templates in Top Producer or a similar database/CRM.

The most crucial element to all this that I stress to every business owner is their ability to evaluate systems and make sure processes run efficiently. This can be extremely helpful in making revisions to your training manual as needed so your business is always being documented and updated. This is essential for when it comes time to pass the training materials on to the next pupil.

I hope that was a great overview. Now let's dive into the nitty gritty of each one so you can see how their presence adds real value to our real estate business.

Sample Schedule of One of Our VAs

I thought it would be helpful to go ahead and include a sample schedule of what one of our virtual assistants does for us on a daily basis so you can see the level of breakdown and how we are able to track everything they do. This level of detail is important because it allows the virtual assistant to stay on track and for us to not only monitor their progress in each task, but to track their success and failures so we can make our systems more efficient for them and our business.

This level of detail takes a while but you start by having your virtual assistants do one task consistently every day. You track it, monitor it, perfect it, and add another task. Once you do that, you add another one and keep going from there. Soon you will have a full calendar like we do, filled with tasks for them to complete in a given day. This allows your virtual assistant to not get overwhelmed and you can see where they are struggling in each task you provide them.

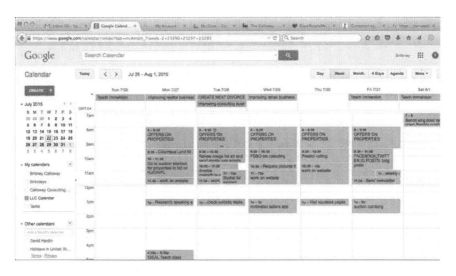

Let's analyze this schedule so you can see a day in the life of our virtual assistant. Every morning they are reviewing all the property leads that have been sent to us the night prior. These are from wholesalers, website leads, calls another virtual assistant received, bandit sign leads, and any other campaign we worked on. All of them have been funneled into our Podio database. Once they have looked at all the offers and sorted out the ones that are not for us, they then go ahead and make offers on all the decent properties and send them to us for review. Specifically, on Monday I also have them looking at the Columbus wholesaler list expressly to get leads from people who put new ones out every Monday.

The next task in the day is looking at auction properties for us. They are scouting the in-person auctions. They are responsible for looking up the information for the county and making sure there are no liens on the properties. They then give all the information to me or a runner that we have in that designated city who is going to go to the auction live in the cities we are investing in and bid for us. They prepare all of the documents and we mail them a packet for them to take to the auction site.

I also have them working on a new website we are putting together as another lead page source for our business. On Tuesday, they are now posting ads on Craigslist and renewing our ads. They are also responding to ads that they find that match our buying criteria. The next hour they are putting together a divorce mailing campaign which is a part of a series of seven touches to a customer for us. The next hour I have them doing a voicemail campaign for motivated For Sale by Owners.

On Wednesday, I have them researching and collecting more numbers for motivated sellers in the area and putting them into a database that will allow us to call them and leave a voicemail saying we are interested in buying their property. The next piece is the newsletter so it is up to her to actually reach out to the contractors each week and ask them for pictures so she can put them in our newsletter. This allows us to keep our lenders updated on all of the projects that we have going on. She is again working on our website and then on a motivated sellers' app that allows you to pull lists for your direct mail campaign.

The next day she is cold calling Realtors who have different projects that fit our criteria and asking them to put us on their buyers' list. She has a script that allows her to speak with them and to sell our business. She is also visiting the squeeze pages to check any leads that we have and making sure our SEO campaign is working and that we are, in fact, getting more leads driven to us and our website.

The next day she is working on our social media. She is using a program I'll mention later on called Hootsuite that allows you to post on all your social media outlets at the same time. During this time she is going to sites we designated and creating posts for every day of the week. Her next task is attending our weekly check-in meeting so that we are able to assess how the week is going, what we need to work on, and how we can improve her experience and our own systems. It is here where I also tell her what the week is looking like, review her progress, and make sure she is hitting all the goals and tasks we asked her to do.

After that she is back to auction scouting and bidding on properties that we told her to watch, as many online final bids are due on a Wednesday or a Friday. She knows exactly how much we want to buy the property for and is scouting and bidding to make sure that we win the property. We have bought quite a few properties off an auction site with our virtual assistants, so this strategy does work for the online auctions.

Chapter 8: VA Social Media Impact

Social Media

If you don't think social media can enhance your business then you are approaching social media incorrectly. We have found deals, lenders, contractors, agents, and networking partners all off social media.

The first step to social media that interns or virtual assistants can help with is building your business presence. People who see that there are a large number of positive comments being made about your company or you as an individual are more likely to do business with you.

The ways to increase likes on Facebook and followers on Twitter and Instagram is to find content that applies to your audience. Therefore we spend a significant amount of time having interns/virtual assistants look up content based on the day of the week. Monday is a time for us to give a motivational or inspirational post. Tuesday is a day for us to write or post an article that engages the Realtor network we are trying to boost. Wednesday and Saturday are targeted to motivated sellers. Thursday is for qualified buyers. Friday is for lenders and Sunday is another all engaging post about real estate.

Our virtual assistants do not need to post directly to our social media pages as there are programs like Hootsuite that allow you to cue up posts for a week. This then allows us to review the content and let our virtual assistant know if there are any tweaks that need to be made.

In addition to social media posts, we have trained our virtual assistants to advertise properties on Facebook through ads. We set open house records on our rehabs every time we advertise our featured listing on Facebook using a targeted search. We have also found interested investors by doing Facebook posts advertising that we can give them a great return on their investment.

When it comes to Instagram and posting pictures of our featured rehabs from the beginning process to the end, we have had numerous sellers contact us about buying their houses via cash from them. We also use the social media outlets to run "background checks" on the people we are doing business with. LinkedIn is a great way to vet our contractors, agents, mortgage lenders, etc. as we start to refer our clients to these different companies for different services and products.

In addition to social media outreach to vet people, we also use LinkedIn and Yahoo! profile groups to build our buyers' and sellers' lists. We have had our virtual assistants comb through these groups in order to build lists of people that we could reach out to about our different projects in order to form new business partnerships. Social media is a powerful method of increasing one's business social presence.

Craigslist is a great way to advertise for selling and buying properties. Virtual assistants can create the ad, post the ad, and monitor the response rate to the ad that was designed. Virtual assistants can also utilize Craigslist as a tool to help you—as a real estate business owner—build your buyers' list through the different ads and groups. Virtual assistants can put the contacts into your database as well as categorize them accordingly. This will help you as you are able to generate more contacts, which creates more leads and closes more deals.

VAs can be responsible for helping you create ads on Facebook, Instagram, Linkedin, and Twitter so that your business can build more presence and leads can be generated. They are also extremely helpful with managing the ads and content you send out via email drip campaigns through autoresponder programs such as Aweber or Mail Chimp and with tracking your response rate through Bananatag and other third party applications.

Specific to Facebook, we have had a few leads come in through the retargeting feature that "follows" a customer who has left our website. Re-targeting then allows for our posts and advertisements to show up on a network of other websites they visit if they leave our site without first opting in by filling out our information form. This campaign is powerful and allows sellers to see that we are still interested even if they did leave our website. We have our virtual assistants run these campaigns for us and, as always, track the response we get to determine which ads work best for us.

Chapter 9: Leads

Leads!

This topic is critical as it relates to real estate! It doesn't get any simpler than this: the more leads you generate, the more deals you will actually close on. For those technicians currently in business, I feel for you because running around trying to turn a lead into a deal can be a lot of work. It is also extremely frustrating when the lead you spent hours on doesn't work out and falls through. In our business we have systems for how we approach generating leads. Therefore, we are able to accurately generate, evaluate, and decide whether to convert leads to deals, wholesale our leads, buy and hold them, or rehab them.

We have virtual assistants who funnel our leads for us. As we use social media, website ads, squeeze and lead pages, direct mail, bandit signs, text marketing, cold calling, market research and other tactics, each lead generation portal has a system behind it. As the leads are generated, they are evaluated by our virtual assistants and presented to us as deals to wholesale, deals to rehab, buy and hold, or list via a Realtor.

In addition, each lead is assigned to the appropriate teammate in order to leverage our time. For example, when a lead comes in to me from New Brunswick, NJ, we already have a Realtor who will run the comps on the lead as well as a contractor who will go see that property for us and let us know the repair estimates. Our virtual assistant then plugs the numbers into a spreadsheet for us and determines if this is a deal worth pursuing. With the sheer volume of leads we receive, I could sit down all day, every day and just analyze deals, which is not a good use of my time. Therefore, it is best to learn this skill, establish your criteria and parameters, and then train someone else to do it for you.

Also, once the address of the lead is taken down and where exactly it came from is put into our database, there is extensive documentation attached to it. We document where each lead came from, when people are contacted, notes on what was said via each email or phone communication as well as dates to follow up and next steps. This way when any of our team members, whether it's a Realtor, other virtual assistant, or a contractor takes a look at the lead, they know exactly where we are in the process of converting the lead into a deal.

It is important to document everything especially as it relates to the contact made on each lead because it the responsibility of our virtual assistants to keep a follow-up timeline to make sure we are there to catch the seller when a deal is HOT and they are finally ready to sell their property. We have been denied on offers, told "not right now" or received "never will call" responses from sellers. However, situations change and people are motivated by different things.

Therefore, we have also had many instances where people call us and are now ready to sell their property based on the numbers we had originally proposed because their buyer fell out of contract, they realized mold does decrease the value of their property, or their Realtor isn't providing them with the best results. The list is endless as to why properties fall out of contract and the price decreases, but it does indeed happen.

This process of turning a lead into a deal is also documented so our virtual assistant can keep track of the progress of other team members. Did the contractor or the Realtor go and see the property and upload the pictures/repair estimate? We monitor the status of each lead so we know exactly where it is in our process of evaluation and going to contract so NO deal falls between the cracks. Every lead that comes in, whether it is via phone, bandit sign, direct mail, Internet, wholesalers, investor meetings, etc., are documented in our system and evaluated thoroughly before we go to closing.

Another piece that I briefly mentioned earlier is the reporting and tracking of leads and where they come from and creating or adjusting our marketing strategies accordingly. Our virtual assistants are responsible for creating a monthly report on our marketing efforts. Each bandit sign is tracked and tallies are created to indicate where each lead comes from and if we should continue or re-strategize where to put our signs. Likewise, virtual assistants are responsible for tracking our direct mail campaigns and reporting how many touches an individual has received with regard to mailings from us, which neighborhoods have been more responsive than others, etc. This allows us to see what we are doing well and what we can expand on as we continue to report our numbers.

Making Calls and Taking Calls

I remember my first really good direct mail campaign that I did and had to take the calls on. This was before my system was in place. I remember trying to use my lunch hour to return sellers' phone calls and I was writing all the info the seller was giving me on a notepad. Not only was I not successful, I wasted an insane amount of valuable time because I was not organized. Once you complete a couple of marketing campaigns in a row, expect to be overwhelmed as your phone will be ringing off the hook. If this happens and you do not have systems in place, you will only cause detriment to your business.

This is why I recommend hiring a virtual assistant who is able to answer your calls and take the leads that come in via the telephone so you can focus on just getting ready for the appointment with the seller and closing the deal. A motivated seller can call our phone 24/7 as there is someone always available to take the call. In addition, the virtual assistant knows the questions to ask our motivated seller, such as who owns the property, how much equity is in the property, when was the last time the roof was fixed or looked at. There are roughly fifty questions our virtual assistants ask a motivated seller when they call us. They then upload that information into Podio, run comps on the house, and write an offer that we should make on the property based on that information.

As you can see from the sample schedule above, we also have our virtual assistants make calls to Realtors, For Sale by Owners, attorneys, other wholesalers, and lenders to get deals as well. This strategy has been extremely beneficial for our company and has resulted in a flood of leads. While this strategy hasn't gotten us a whole lot of rehab projects, it has been lucrative when we needed to wholesale a few deals to get some cash. This strategy is very labor intensive. I recommend calling each business type (Realtor, wholesaler, lender, etc.) on your own and developing a call script for your market, and then have your virtual assistant take over from there.

Acquiring Properties Through the MLS

There are many ways to acquire properties in the real estate industry. One way which many people underestimate is the Multiple Listing Service (MLS). We have our virtual assistant comb through the MLS looking for properties in order to see which ones we should make offers on. They put the offer together, we approve it, and they send it over to the listing agent. They keep track of all the offers made so that we can follow up on the properties that didn't take our offer the first time. They also comb through the MLS for expired listings and create a list for us to use for either a direct mail campaign or cold calling. Moreover, they are able to pull the pre-foreclosure, 30, 60, and 90 day foreclosure list. They have been able to direct us and help us build buyers and sellers for free and clear properties, For Sale By Owner, and short sale clients.

While the MLS is a great tool for making offers, tracking listings, and building lists, it is not the only tool to acquire properties. Our virtual assistants are also helpful in gathering all the documents together for Dotloop (for my real estate agents) for a property to be listed on the MLS. They can provide the property details, organize the photo shoot, collect the photos, and create a new MLS entry each time there is a new property assignment, as well as publicize the MLS entry on all the necessary databases in order to circulate the listing through different outlets. They can also aid in the listing to have a social media presence through virtual tours, your website, and your YouTube channel.

Chapter 10: Assisting in Real Estate Finance

Transactions

The actual mechanics of a real estate transaction are a key part of investing that must go smoothly. Virtual assistants can play a huge role in this. Their responsibilities can include coordinating with the Escrow Officer, a lender, and managing expenses on projects to make sure payments are made timely and efficiently.

With regard to escrow accounts, our virtual assistants coordinate with the escrow office to make sure payments are there to meet the deadline needed for closing. They are also responsible for coordinating payouts with the escrow agent to make sure lenders are paid back in addition to us if we are not able to make a closing. With regard to hard-money lenders (though I haven't had to use hard money on a deal just yet), our assistants would be responsible for making the monthly payments and managing the monthly payouts.

The virtual assistant who acts as a project manager for a specific rehab project is also responsible for managing the transactions that take place for each project. This process entails managing the payment schedule that our contractors are on for the specific project and checking the benchmarks as outlined in the contract to make sure we are paying for the specific work done. We have found it is helpful for our virtual assistants to remind our contractors that they should expect a check on Friday if "the following items" are completed as outlined in our contract.

This also includes tracking all expenses incurred by the project that the contractor or we submit and recording it in QuickBooks. At the end of the rehab, the virtual assistant is able to tell us exactly how much was spent per project so we know how to save on future expenses. We always have an estimated profit that we anticipate on making but having a virtual assistant over this allows us to know exactly how much profit we ended up making on each deal.

The virtual assistant also helps us look up pricing at different stores for different materials that we may need so that we don't have to go to three different building supply stores to pick out the product. Our assistant can locate it for us ahead of time, make sure it's in stock, and coordinate for the contractor or a runner to go pick it up.

QuickBooks

Speaking of transactions, documenting your business expenses is VITAL to the success of your real estate business. When documenting my expenses for the year for tax time, it took me an hour a week to complete QuickBooks. I was doing my best to update all the expenses I made for the week regarding my business and categorizing them accordingly as well as making sure documentation for contractors was also made appropriately.

Now that a virtual assistant is assigned to this task, I will never do it again as it was my least favorite part of the business— though it is without a doubt the most important one as well.

The system for this looks as follows. We take pictures of the receipt or the charge and note what it was for as well as write down the code letters representing what it should be categorized as in QuickBooks. From there, our virtual assistants are responsible for entering that data into QuickBooks under the appropriate file. I.e., a dinner with business partners will be labeled on the receipt {M} business meeting with partners. Our virtual assistant knows to put that in the section classified for meals and will document the amount, date of the transaction, and what it was for in QuickBooks.

They are also responsible for documenting our loans, interest made, as well as keeping track of the HUD documents needed for tax purposes. This saves us an incredible amount of time and allows us to do other tasks. When it comes to tax time our assistant then works with our tax preparer to make sure all documentation is provided, such as receipts for large items, W-9 for contractors, mileage tracker for our business travel, etc. This documentation is given to our tax preparer, which has saved us thousands of dollars in business expenses. As a disclaimer, we do block out specific account information, credit card numbers and Social Security numbers when giving this to our virtual assistant to work from.

QuickBooks is not free (we have a business account with them) but it is worth its weight in gold as documenting all of these expenses has saved us time and has absolutely allowed us to reduce our taxes.

Hiring

This may sound like a weird topic to discuss. How can a virtual assistant help us hire other virtual assistants, general contractors, or subcontractors? Well, they can and have helped us hire the best of the best in the industry. For hiring contractors specifically, they are responsible for the bulk of the hiring process and we come in at the very end.

They are responsible for advertising, reviewing each initial application, checking documentation, the initial interview questionnaire, as well as setting up times for the contractors to see the job. Once the job post has been released, our virtual assistants are responsible for combing through the initial batch of applications/ documentation. This allows us to go from 15 contractor applications to four once the virtual assistants discard the applications that weren't 100% completed.

The virtual assistant then goes through the initial questionnaire with them on a recorded line that we listen to and schedules a final interview in person for us to review their entire package. Contractors are then notified by our virtual assistant of the project and are told to visit it and give us a project proposal. The VA also helps us to create a scope of work and then sends it over to the Realtor so that she can place the scope of work paperwork in the actual house. Contractors then visit the house, pick up the scope of work and place their bids on the project. The bids are then given to us and we tell the virtual assistant which ones we would like to set up a phone interview with.

As you can see, I just laid out the steps of hiring individuals and it is obvious that we don't even have to do any work until the final interviews are conducted. We are then responsible for reviewing the final portfolios, calling the references, meeting in person to walk them through all of our documents, and making the final decisions on our contractors.

When it comes to hiring virtual assistants or other team members, the process is identical. They can do a lot of the initial screening and put together a package including work experience and references, and make sure everything is in order with the applicant. We review the package and then make our final decision. They can also help with on-boarding them by making sure we have their DropBox accounts set up. We have email accounts set up for our VAs, storing all their paperwork, etc.

Send Emails

I think it is important as a business owner to respond to emails in as timely a manner as possible. With our virtual assistants, we have now allowed them to answer emails for us. They are able to log in and see what is personal, what needs immediate attention, and what can wait. We don't allow them to access our personal email, just our business accounts so that business clients are able to have responses in 24 hours. In addition, we have them send emails from our business accounts on a drip campaign or follow up campaign so that we are able to capture all leads that were a no the first time around.

Text Message Marketing

This is an excellent marketing strategy in today's market. Studies show that only 10 percent of the people you email will actually open your emails on a campaign, but 98 percent will open and read a text message. This is a huge marketing strategy to take advantage of.

We have our virtual assistants compile lists of numbers for absentee owners, tax liens, and For Sale by Owners, and have them text our hot leads letting them know that we are interested in buying their house.

There are plenty of text marketing apps that you have to pay monthly to send the text messages. We have used Ez Texting to send messages to motivated sellers letting them know that we are interested in buying their house. It also allows us to do a text campaign follow up if they did not respond the first time.

Expired Listings

Another marketing campaign that we have our virtual assistants implement for us is combing through the expired listings on Zillow, Trulia, and a few of the other prominent sites to find leads. Our virtual assistants are able to comb through and put together a list of properties that are expired and could use another offer from someone like us. It may be an offer we made the first time and they said no, and the second time they may say yes.

This is why it is always important to follow up. We have our virtual assistants use this strategy so that we are able to capture more leads and let motivated sellers know that we are still willing to work with them. We may even increase our offer price the second time around to show that we are dedicated and committed to buying their house.

Direct Mail

This is another strategy that we use which is essential to leads that come our way. The average number of touches you need to make nowadays for people to feel comfortable in trusting your company is closer to 12 to 15 versus the five to seven average touches that were effective in the '80s and '90s. We use our direct mail campaigns to get personal with our potential customers, to show them what we are about, how we are able to help them, and that we will put their needs first. We make sure we highlight testimonials of other people who have worked with us and have been successful. We also make sure we highlight our signature programs that separate us from other investors that I mentioned earlier in our business model.

We show people the advantages of working with an investor versus working with a Realtor and how we can help them by creating a better trajectory for their life overall—not just through one sale. In our marketing campaigns, we also want to make sure we add a personal touch and do different touches each time. We send post cards, letters, handwritten letters, a plan for their house, "why" invest with us—the list is and should be endless. You also shouldn't be afraid to try something new. It is vitally important to document and track the response rate for each piece and that is where our virtual assistants come into play.

We take the time to create each individual marketing piece, however we have our virtual assistants track the response rate to see what pieces we should keep, tweak, and try for next time. I have also included a sample of a direct mail marketing piece that could be used to target a foreclosure list. This is just a sample and should be tweaked for your market, with your company's programs, and your information, but it is helpful to see what can be done:

Top Notch Property Solutions
Real Estate Solutions Company

Top Notch Property Solutions, Inc. is the DMV's premier real estate solutions company located in the heart of Washington D.C. Our company specializes in solving complex real estate problems. Since the beginning, our company has helped hundreds of home-

owners. Whether you are looking to stay in the home or sell we can provide a quick and easy solution. Our company specializes in foreclosure avoidance and we are the foremost expert in this arena. We can help stop the foreclosure and avoid bankruptcy in most scenarios. We work with each homeowner individually and explore all possible options.

Additionally, the company has helped numerous families achieve the dream of home ownership through its first time home buyer educational program and credit repair program.

We are a member of the Better Business Bureau and have been an integral part of the community for years. We can provide numerous references from past clients upon request.

Call us today and we can discuss your options! (Phone Number)

Purchase Programs

In many instances it may be in your best interest to sell. If you are struggling to make the mortgage payment each month you may need or want to find a more affordable situation. Likewise, do not risk losing valuable equity to a pending foreclosure by not taking action. We can purchase your home directly from you and there are no hefty Realtor commissions you will have to pay. We can also close very quickly or on your timeline, whatever you prefer. Call us today and we can make you an offer in less than 24 hours!

Mortgage Refinance Programs

If saving your home is your goal we can help! We work with many national lenders who specialize in refinancing homeowners who are behind on payments. Most mortgage companies will shy away from borrowers with tarnished credit, but not the lenders we work with. We will work diligently to find the best loan product for you. If this program interests you, please speak with us today because the longer you delay, the more difficult it will be to qualify!

Loan Modification Programs

A "Loan Modification Program" is a special program designed to help homeowners who had a previous hardship get back on track with their mortgage. We will work directly with you and your lender to help you qualify, however you must have recovered from that hardship, and be able to make your mortgage payments again. Often times the lender will require some sort of partial payment before they will consider a loan modification program. The relationships we have built with many banks will help you immensely during this process.

Short Sale Programs

With today's declining real estate market, it can be very difficult for some homeowners to sell their property. If you are overleveraged, you may be tempted to just walk away. However, this is not in your best interest. There are serious consequences if you let the home go to foreclosure. If this is a scenario you are currently experiencing you must understand you have options. We are very successful at negotiating debt with banks and can often times purchase your property directly from you thus saving you from a foreclosure.

Credit Repair Programs

Whether you are looking to repair your credit from an unfortunate financial event or improve your credit score in order to purchase another home in the future, our network of credit repair specialists can produce results quickly. We can provide educational materials, step-by-step instruction, and professional credit coaching throughout the course of a year to help you right the ship and get back on track.

Homeowner Relocation Programs

We realize the challenges homeowners face when selling their property. That is why we created the Homeowner Relocation Program run by _____ who will work hand in hand with you to locate another home or an apartment depending on your needs. They can also arrange for movers if this is something you desire. We know selling a home can be stressful and believe in going the extra mile for our customers. Please inquire about the program and let us help you with your transition.

Company Testimonials

"Being in the mortgage business, I know how complicated home transactions can be and that is why I have been so impressed with the way Top Notch does business. I have seen them solve some of the most difficult real estate problems that other investors and real estate professionals would not touch. If you are looking to refinance, sell, or buy a home I would deal with them first!"

- Mike Washington, Mortgage Broker

"I had a very complicated Real Estate problem whereby I owed much more than my house was worth and as a result could not sell my property. You actually negotiated my debt down with my mortgage company and were able to purchase my house thus saving me from foreclosure."

- Chris Connor, Home Seller

"I cannot thank your company enough for helping me solve my real estate problems. I was behind on my mortgage and needed someone to close quickly. The company actually made up all of my back payments and continued to pay my mortgage which has helped me re-establish my credit. I cannot thank you enough."

- Shareef H., Home Seller

Once you are able to create all the "touch" materials, you or the virtual assistants can send them to a mail fulfillment company and have your virtual assistants initiate and monitor the campaign. You can then have them track each list, delete addresses that were sent back, monitor which campaign pulled the most responses, and have them take phone calls for you from the return calls, and, of course, enter the leads into Podio.

Online Data Entry

As stated before, it is important to track campaigns, offers, ads—basically everything! If it has a system, it can be tracked and improved upon. They told me as a teacher the most important thing I could do was track my students' data. How would I know the possibilities in a child's growth if I didn't know where they started? In order to see growth in my students' test scores I had to know where they were, have a system/plan in place, have benchmarks to make sure there was progress, and of course, an end goal. This concept that I learned straight out of college in my teaching days still very much applies to my business today.

Knowing where my business stands at all times allows me to know how it can be improved upon. Therefore, it is important that we track every marketing campaign by using Excel, a paid provider, or a database to track our data and let us know where we can improve. Our virtual assistants are able to report to us the number of offers made in a given week, how many calls we received from direct mail campaigns, how many people we emailed in a follow-up campaign, how many people actually read our emails, how many deals we closed on, how close we were to our rehab budget, how much money we have raised to date, etc. The list is truly endless.

These key things aforementioned are important to track because each month we have a new goal that we are trying to hit. Being able to accurately track our data enables us to set new benchmarks, which makes it easier to reach our end goals. I hear too many people say they want to do twenty successful flips in one year but have not thought of the systems needed, or the data they need to track to make sure they achieve their goals. This will always be a hindrance and at some point you will become stagnant if you do not track your business systems and campaigns.

Website

In 2015, we know it is key to have an online presence. People now use the internet to do a background check on you and see what people have to say about you and your business. Therefore, it is important to make sure your online presence is an accurate reflection of how you do business. We have our virtual assistants help us so that we are able to continue to show others the quality work that we do.

You can pay a company to do your website but you want to make sure that you have a virtual assistant who can add content and maintain the website for you. I had a virtual assistant set up my personal website. Your best bet is to use a WordPress site. Make sure you pick a good website domain name. You can use GoDaddy.com to buy the name and, once you have it, you can give access to your virtual assistant who can start to create the pages on your website. It's always best to try to get a "dot com" web address if you can. It's also often worth buying the .net/.org/.edu and other variations and setting up a redirect to your dot com site so no one else can take that domain name. It's fairly inexpensive to have those three for the year so it is best to buy them.

There are a lot of web developer virtual assistants that are trained and will do a good job. The key is vetting them and checking on the projects that they have actually completed. In my experience, web developers can often be unreliable and hard to get hold of, so be clear when hiring by telling them exactly what you want, the timeframe and the budget—and find out exactly what will and won't be included in those costs. It is also important ahead of time to do your homework on what you want.

Make sure you look at different sites as comparisons and show the developer exactly what you want. It is also important to make sure you have the content written out in advance so they are ready to go and aren't waiting on you for action items. It is important to decide on the design, colors, content, and amount of pages ahead of time. Make sure the site is easy to navigate and that it is not too cluttered and hard to find the valuable information you are trying to convey. Make sure your main page attracts all of the audiences you think will be visiting your site on a daily basis.

In addition, we paid a copywriter to look over all of the content that we put on our site to make sure there were no spelling or grammatical errors. It is easy to miss them when you are writing things for your own site. It is also vital to have testimonials on your website of different people who tried your services and benefited from them. If you don't have any, then get some by doing an hour of free work or skill swap with another business owner to get some in order to build credibility.

It is also essential to blog on your website. Many people find it time consuming, but that is what you can hire a virtual freelance writer or a virtual assistant to do for you. When you blog, you drive traffic to your site and gain more leads. These articles don't need to be novels. They are a way to demonstrate your expertise on particular subjects and showcase studies of deals you've come across so that these new clients can fully see all that you have to offer. Remember blogs should be informational and have purpose. I have seen too many people waste time writing irrelevant blog articles and wonder why no traffic is being driven to their site. It is important to be purposeful with blogs; if not, then don't blog.

It is also important to link your social media to your websites. One caveat: if you do tie your Facebook, Linkedin, Twitter, and Instagram to your webpage, be sure they are purely reflective of your *professional* business and not your personal life. I have one social media account for my personal endeavors as well as an account for my business. We have all seen controversies arise when people on their business page share their personal feelings which causes people to learn a little bit more about you versus the business that you are trying to promote. It is your page and your choice however, I know many clients who will not do business with people based on what they saw on their social media accounts.

Your website MUST be search engine optimized (SEO). When I first made my website I was confused as to why I wasn't getting leads instantaneously. However, it later made sense. What is the point of having a website if Google doesn't know it exists and it doesn't come up when someone searches for the site? Therefore, it is important to make sure you are constantly plugging your website on different outlets so that you can get traffic to it and get leads.

There is a great free plug in called WordPress SEO for those using WordPress that allows you to optimise all of the pages and posts that you have by allowing you to write your own meta descriptions and keywords. This is essential as you develop your targeted audience. Once you think like they do, you are able to create keywords that your targeted audience may type in to find a site like yours.

The more times this site is visited, the more your website rises in the search engine world and goes from being on the third or fourth page in a search to the first. You can also tell Google to track data for you by registering your website's site map with Google. Google will then give you an alert if there are any problems with it. Google Analytics can also be added to your site and will track how people are finding you and what your most popular pages are. This is a huge asset as you can then boost articles that a large amount of people are interested in to others to gain more visitors to your site. It also lets you know where people are finding you so that you can continue to boost your site to the different outlets where you are getting the most traction.

We have our virtual assistants monitor this process for us. They are particularly skilled in web development so we can see exactly where and who we are getting leads from and how we can continue to boost our site and gain more traction and leads into our database. We also make sure our virtual assistant is updating our website at least once a month with different information so that we aren't keeping it stagnant but constantly adding to it. It is once again important to be clear in what your goals are for your site with your virtual assistant so you can set benchmarks and make sure you are constantly growing your online presence.

The best ways to get traction to your website are to do the following: put your business on Google local so you come up in local searches for your business category, register the site on a ton of local business directories, add a blog, make short videos of different tutorials for your business to gain traction, feature different properties and deals on your website, use Google Adwords which is also great for using keywords in your market, and just networking and sending out blasts about the site so people can word of mouth your services, as well.

Lead Pages

Online marketing tools are essential to our business and in helping us bring in leads. In order to do this we have created what is called squeeze pages or lead pages that are attached to specific keywords. For instance, we have a foreclosure lead page in our Ohio market. When someone clicks on Google and types in foreclosure and Ohio they will see our squeeze page come up. Once on our page, they can type in their property address to get an estimate of what their house may be worth based on the foreclosure process. These lead pages/squeeze pages are very helpful as it allows you to generate more leads.

They are also very easy to set up. You can go to HostMonster.com or GoDaddy.com to pick the domain name. We then have our virtual assistants upload the content that we have given them. They are also responsible for linking each lead page with our Podio database so that no leads go un-captured or undocumented. From there, the Podio process starts, which allows our VAs to run the numbers and estimate the value of the property and formulate an offer, as well as tell us if it is a good deal or not.

Wholesale

Wholesaling in real estate, as we define it, is the process of acquiring the contract on a property from a seller and assigning it to a buyer. Wholesaling can be its own full time business as there are plenty of people who make six figures just doing wholesale deals alone. Moreover, having virtual assistants help your wholesale business will only grow your business nationally. In our business, we get a ton of leads and are at the point where we no longer have to take the deals that are under a $50,000 profit.

Therefore, we like to wholesale those deals to other investors. How we do that is by making sure our virtual assistants are constantly building our buyers' list of investors, lenders, Realtors, and cash buyers who may be interested in the property we don't want. This allows us to still make a profit and not rehab all the houses we get under contract. Our virtual wholesaling business is easier than one thinks to run. Essentially, we follow a detailed checklist that our virtual assistants help us manage.

Podio

There should be a whole book on Podio as there are so many ways it has helped our business, all for the cost of $Free. Podio is the database that we use to store all of our leads. It allows us to work with our virtual assistants to create checklists for every step of the process so that they do not get confused, monitor their progress, run numbers on our systems, and tweak any changes.

Once you get on Podio and set up a free account, I would reference Charles Blair's YouTube video and cheat sheet on how to get your Podio set up. Our VA followed all of the steps and turned our system into a money-making machine. This is where all of our important contacts are stored. This is where all of our leads funnel in and where we can track where we are with each lead. In addition, we have all of our team members in Podio, which makes our life easier.

Once the leads have been sent to our Podio system, our virtual assistant will go in, run the numbers, and put an offer for them in Podio based on running the comps and using the Maximum Allowable Offer (MAO) formula to assess what we should be offering. Depending on the list we mailed to (i.e., pre-foreclosure or expired listings), we are going to call them back immediately to make an offer on their house and try to schedule a time to sit down with them. We may let our virtual assistant call them and set up a time to meet with us or make a verbal offer on the phone to them.

As you can see, this takes off a lot of time for us. We are only responsible for checking the numbers to see if the offer makes sense and sitting down in person with the client to get the deal under contract.

For example, once an offer has been drafted by our virtual assistant we can "assign the task" in Podio, which is an alert to our teammate who is our Realtor to submit the offer. Now that we have a property under contract, we can "assign the task" to our contractor to go give us a full estimate of the repairs. Adding our team members allows everyone to be on the same page and lets us know where we are in the process for every lead that comes our way. In addition, Podio allows you to do complete email campaigns, and can be the database for where all your online and offline leads come in.

Our virtual assistant who manages our Podio is also able to track everything someone does and reports to us the status of where we are with each lead, contact, marketing campaigns, offer, wholesale, or rehab. Podio has also been great for allowing us to document where we are in each step of our wholesale and rehab so the ball doesn't get dropped and each team member knows what they should be doing. Once you have your Podio up and running, and it is truly running for you, you won't go back to paying for a database ever again.

Just to provide the specifics in what we use...

For our email follow-up campaigns that we use through Podio, we use MailChimp to deliver the emails to the people we are trying to do business with. We do this for sellers, Realtors, contractors, and especially lenders. Mail Chimp is fantastic since it is free and allows you to send what is called a "drip" email campaign to prospective clients for business. Our VA is very skilled in campaigns so we let her design the emails for our target market, we approve the campaign, and then she will send the campaign out every week or every month depending on who we are targeting.

vCita

I am a fan of vCita because it allows my virtual assistants to manage my contacts and my calendar. Every week, I go in and block off times that I am available to speak to someone. I also tell my virtual assistant weekly who I would like them to reach out to on my behalf so I can get them on the phone to discuss business. This tactic eliminates the back and forth emails between each party to find a time that works.

This way you can manage your time via your calendar online versus trying to write down all of your appointments. In addition, you can fire yourself from this task so you can free your time up to do more of the entrepreneurial tasks. The app will also sync with your phone and your Google calendar so that you can set reminders of when your meetings are with your clients.

The best part about vCita is that it is free. The business account is also fairly inexpensive and allows you to create invoices for your business, manage all of your contacts, and will even give you 24 hour support staff for whatever needs may arise in your business. vCita is an excellent tool to consider especially if your volume starts to get higher in terms of meeting with sellers, lenders, Realtors, contractors, etc. Managing your time is truly the most important aspect of your business and vCita will help with that task.

Conclusion

Why Is It Important to Outsource Now?

I always say time isn't just money in business: it is truly everything. The quicker you can duplicate yourself and give your lower-prioritized tasks to someone else, the more free time you have to work on ideas, growth, and production in your business. I listened to a panel on Millionaire Investing and the moderator stated that 85% of millionaires say their biggest year of growth came from hiring their first employee. If you start outsourcing now you will without a doubt start to fire yourself so that you can move up the ranks in your business.

How You Can Outsource Tomorrow!

My final recommendation is to hire your first virtual assistant! If you call myoutdesk.com and say Brittney Calloway referred you, you will get a significant discount off your initial set-up fee. Once you have hired your virtual assistant, it is best to get them trained on everything in your business. This requires you to document all your business practices at an eighth grade level so that your assistants can understand exactly what you would like them to accomplish.

If I had to pick the top three areas to outsource for real estate immediately, it would be my phone, putting offers in for me, and my marketing campaigns. Those free up your time drastically, especially in the real estate business. This allows you to once again climb the ladder so that you are working on being the entrepreneur and not the technician in your business.

Our Consulting Course

Brittney Calloway offers a six month virtual course teaching you and your virtual assistants how she automates her business. Her course comes with over 20 hours of instructional webinar content, monthly coaching calls, and a training manual that you can customize for your business. You can sign up to learn more about it at www.reiautomationcourse.com/form or schedule a consultation with Brittney Calloway at www.vcita.com/v/topnotchconsulting

We hope you thoroughly enjoyed this book and wish you great success in your REI automation journey.

APPENDIX

Helpful Worksheets in Your Journey with Virtual Assistants

Menu for Virtual Assistant Tasks

Place a check next to systems in your businesses that already exist. Place a star next to the top three priorities or areas of weakness where you need help.

_____ Email Management/Filtering

_____ Setting up Autoresponders (Aweber, MailChimp)

_____ Booking appointments with Sellers/Realtors/buyers/ attorneys

_____ Follow up with clients/customers (send thank yous and other reminder emails)

_____ Receptionist duties (answering occasional calls)

_____ Calendar Management

_____ File Management (organizing files using Dropbox, etc.)

_____ Database building (e.g., updating email or contact lists on your CRM)

_____ Research on certain topics for blog posts, newsletters, or others

_____ Managing accounting tasks, i.e., QuickBooks

_____ Transcription (transcribing voicemail, video or audio, podcasts, etc.)

_____ Creating basic reports (reports on weekly tasks, deliverables, sales)

_____ Presentation material such as slideshows/documents

_____ Investor collateral (loan request packages)

_____ Social Media set up (Facebook, Twitter, LinkedIn, YouTube)

_____ Social Media management and posting

_____ Manage your blog (Basic WordPress Skills)

_____ Publish posts on your blog (content you provided)

_____ Manage bandit signs/door knocking/pink slip campaigns

_____ Managing your rehab projects (project management)

_____ Managing communication between sub-contractors

_____ Generating website leads

_____ Conducting/tracking direct mail campaigns

Time Commitment for Outsourcing Business tasks

You can get 10 hours of return from an employee for every hour you commit to working with them. How many 10 hour blocks do you want done for you by others?

1. Identify how much time you have each **day** to commit to outsourcing.

We have found that for every 2-3 hours of quality training time we spend with our VAs, their efficiency, their quality of output and performance increase by about 3-5%.

2. How much time could you devote to training/following up with your VA each **week**?

3. How many hours could be set aside each of these days? Write down times for each day.

SUN	MON	TUES	WED	THU	FRI	SAT

4. How does this vary depending on the time of year?

5. Based on vacations/conferences/school/work/children, which months will be crucial for a VA? Which months can you be hands on to train/expand/automate new tasks?

JAN	FEB	MAR	APR	MAY	JUNE

JULY	AUG	SEPT	OCT	NOV	DEC

Basic Business Budget Worksheet

If you don't take care of today, there's no reason to focus on tomorrow. Let's make sure your today counts. Spend 1-2 hours max defining your basic budget so you can see how much costs will be.

Category	Budget Amount	Actual Amount	Difference
Revenue			
Interest Income			
Investment Income			
Other Income			
Total Income			
Expenses			
Accounting Services			
Advertising/Marketing			
Bank Service Charges			
Credit Card Fees			
Travel/Hotel/Conf. Fees			
Deposits for Utilities			
Estimated Taxes			
Health Insurance			
Hiring Costs for Virtual Assistants			

Meals and Entertainment			
Interest on Debt			
Calling/Answering Service/Website Maintenance			
Legal Expenses			
Licensing/Permits			
Loan Payments			
Office Supplies			
Foreign File/Trust/LLC Fees			
Printing			
Professional Fees			
Rent/Lease Payments			
Retirement Contributions			
Subscriptions and Dues			
Utilities and Telephone			
Vehicle Expenses			
Other			
Other			
Total Expenses			
Total Income minus Total Expenses			

Budget Worksheet Part II – Follow Up Questions

1. What tasks will you pay by the hour and which tasks will you pay on a project-based schedule?

2. What will your pay schedule look like for project-based VAs?

3. What will your pay schedule look like for hourly-based VAs?

4. How many VAs or interns do you plan on having? What will be the breakdown of tasks for each VA?

5. What will be some of the incentives/bonuses that you will offer to your VAs and interns to help motivate them?

Communication Worksheet with VA

Goal Setting with VA

1. What are the goals that you want to communicate to your VA?

2. How will you describe why the VA is doing what they are doing?

3. What are the VA's goals?

4. How can you assure that you are going to help the VA reach their goals?

Expectation Worksheet

1. When will your team meeting be weekly with your assistant?

2. What will the deadline of projects be?

3. When mistakes are made by your assistant how will you address them?

4. Have you taught your assistant all the steps needed for her/him to be successful?

First Implementation of System Review

1. What was done successfully by the VA? Compliment them first.

2. What things need to be tweaked to be better?

3. How should the VA go about changing the things that need to be changed?

4. What things can be improved to the system to enhance your business even more?

5. Do you need new VAs or can things be negotiated with the current VA so that you can pay more and they can do more?

With Phone Call VAs

1. How is their communication with the seller, buyer, or agent?

2. Are they using the right terms?

3. Are they asking the right questions/delivering the pitch correctly?

Troubleshooting When Problems Occur

1. With things you taught them step-by-step, go back and do the "I do, we do, you do" model.

2. With phone calls, have the VAs listen to one of your recordings. Have you practiced with them? Are the scripts accurate and reflect all the questions that they will possibly get?

3. Go back into your system/manual where your process is written and watch the VA do each step. At what part are they having trouble? How can you communicate the steps they are falling apart on better?

I wanted to provide you with a list of the apps and tools we use with our virtual assistants that have been the most successful.

Founded back in 2008, **Hootsuite** is a popular social media dashboard that enables you to post, monitor, and measure your social media sites. Hootsuite gives you instant and convenient access to all of your social media channels as well as providing analytics to help you best increase your following and traffic. Hootsuite is available to download on iOS and Android devices.

The official **Facebook** app is the long reigning, most downloaded social networking app on both Android and iOS. Geared toward giving users the same experience of using Facebook on their mobile devices as on the website, the Facebook app makes it easy to stay connected and share information with colleagues on portable devices. This is a handy app if you're using Facebook as one of your main social media channels for your business as you can share status updates and content with your followers on the move.

The Facebook app is available to download on both iOS and Android.

Twitter and Google + also have their own social media apps.

WordPress is the most popular blogging tool for personal and business use. With its easy-to-use apps, you can update your blog via smartphone or tablet, upload and edit posts as well as manage user comments on the move. Wordpress can be downloaded from the App Store or Google Play.

Blogger, one of the original blogging tools, but less in vogue today, Blogger makes blogging on the go simple. Update your blog from your smartphone or tablet, upload and edit posts as well as manage user comments on the move. Uploading photos from your device is easy and location services allow geo tags to share your location. Blogger can be downloaded from the App Store or Google Play.

The **LinkedIn** app gives you a useful communication tool that will keep you up to speed with your professional network. Stay up to date with your LinkedIn connections; follow industry influencers to receive regular insights and professional content and search for fellow LinkedIn users, companies and groups and access your LinkedIn messages.

LinkedIn is an effective platform for maintaining professional relationships and posting content, such as recent blog posts, that draws attention towards your business or service. The app is available to download on both iOS and Android.

DropBox allows you to store, sync, and share folders online on a straightforward interface. Use the DropBox app to store photos, videos and documents, and access them anytime and anywhere with an internet connection.

You have the option to share DropBox files with colleagues and other contacts, allowing file sharing for remote marketing teams. DropBox is available for download on both Google Play and Apple App Store.

Many digital marketing agencies now use **Google Drive** in place of DropBox. Like DropBox, you can sync Google Drive with your phone and you can share documents with colleagues. The app gives you access to all your files on any mobile device as well as being able to invite others to view, edits or comment on any of your stored files.

DropBox and Google Drive are available to download from both Google Play and Apple App Store.

AnalyticsPro 2 allows you to view 61 reports organized into eight sections: Summary, Visitors, Traffic Sources, Content, Goals, E-Commerce, App Tracking and Social. Optimized for the iPhone and iPad, you can authenticate the app to access more than one Google account and effortlessly switch between them. Reports can then be emailed as a PDF file and the app allows you to export data to a Text file. Use AnalyticsPro 2 to identify trends and get the most out of Google Analytics on the go.

AnalyticsPro 2 is available to download for about $8 on iOS from Apple App Store.

Earlier this year Google launched the official Google Analytics app, allowing you to access all web and app data on the move. The app is now available to download from both Google Play and App Store.

This list of apps is not conclusive and we would love to hear which apps you find useful when it comes to running your day-to-day digital life.

Made in the USA
Charleston, SC
23 October 2015